The Covenant Woman

The Covenant Woman

SHAYLA GORDON

Library of Congress
Library of Congress Control Number: 2022903571
ISBN Paperback 979-8-9858347-0-3
ISBN ePUB 979-8-9858347-1-0

Printed in the United States of America

ACKNOWLEDGMENTS

I would like to thank those who have supported me in the writing of this prayer guide. My mom, Danita, who has always encouraged me and reminds me I can do anything God has called me to do. Thank you, mom, for being an obedient woman who has taught me so much about standing in faith. My beautiful daughter, Kassidy, who was the first to read this prayer guide. Thank you, sweet girl for joining in on my excitement to do what God has called me to do! My hope is that I make you proud. My twin sister, Shanda, who supports everything I do and who told me she wants the first copy. I would also like to thank every woman in my life. As I was writing this book, I had you in my heart. Whether we are close and talk daily or don't talk often at all, your face flashed through my mind at some point in the writing of this prayer guide. I love you all so much, and I'm incredibly inspired by each of you.

I dedicate this prayer guide to all of you, and to each woman who reads it.

Because I'm a covenant woman, I can have what God says I can have, I can be who God says I can be, and I can do what God says I can do.

"You all have crowns because you were all born into royalty, but oftentimes you allow the guilt from your bad choices or the opinions of others hinder you from seeing it. If you don't make mindset changes and start walking uprightly, you will never grab a hold of the royalty you were born into, but it is there waiting for you."

A word from God, February 2020.

Dear Heavenly Father,

I thank you for the woman reading this book. I ask that you touch her and bless her in all areas of her life including spiritually, physically, financially, emotionally, and relationally. Father, hear her heart with each request she makes known to you. Fill her with peace, patience, wisdom, and guidance in every situation she is in currently, and will go through in the future. Strengthen her faith like never before and guide each step she takes from this moment forward. I ask that you remove the toxic and fill her life with your blessings. Reveal to her things you want her to know. God, I ask that you guide her thoughts, her words, and her actions. Give her a strong desire to spend time with you daily. Raise her up to fulfill the carefully designed life that you have specifically created her for and remind her she is never alone. When the enemy tries to attack any area of her life, remind her she is in a <u>Blood-Covenant</u> with you and has authority over every thought that enters her mind and her every trial that comes her way. When she makes mistakes, help her to not stray from you but instead come boldly to you asking for forgiveness and remain strong in her faith. I claim Romans 8:28 over her life which tells us, *"… we know that all things work together for good to them that love God, to them who are called according to* his *purpose."*

Let your light shine through her so that others see you when they see her. Thank you, Father, that you are a respecter of faith, and you are a keeper of your promises.

In the precious name of Jesus I pray,

Amen

TABLE OF CONTENTS

WHAT'S IN THIS BOOK FOR ME?

The purpose of this prayer guide is to inspire you to step fully into the covenant promises God has promised you by learning the truth about who you are and what belongs to you as a Covenant Woman. Every word from God is a promise, and in Him there is absolutely no lie. If God says you can have it, Sister, you can count on it being yours! However, God saying something belongs to you does not cause it to come to pass in your life. *Your faith activates* God's promises. As a Covenant Woman, it is important to continually be developing your faith. You do this by making God your number one priority. You put His word in your ears and in front of your eyes consistently. As you grow in your faith and your relationship with God, you'll have a deeper understanding of your covenant rights and all the blessings that are available to you.

Are you tired of wondering if God hears your prayers? Are you exhausted wondering why you don't see your prayers being answered? Praying isn't enough to have the life God wants you to have. Did you know to get your prayers answered, it's more than simply asking God to do it? It's about having a relationship with Him, having faith in His promises, and being obedient to His direction. You have the responsibility to believe in what you are praying for. Your faith moves God. Your *faith mixed with God's promises* is how you get your prayers answered. If we can interrupt God's blessings with our lack of faith, think about the mountains in our lives we can move with the increase of our faith!

I don't know about you, but the older I get, the more I do not want any relationship in my life to be lukewarm. Not my friendships, not a romantic relationship, and most certainly not my relationship with God. Lukewarm means average. I don't want my life to be average, and I bet you don't either! God says you can be prosperous in all areas of your life which contradicts a lukewarm lifestyle. In this book, I will teach you what I've learned about how to get prayers answered. A step-by-step guide, if you will, of what to do and what not to do. As you're reading this book, I want you to know that I only wrote what God put on my heart to write. These are His words, and He simply used me as a vessel to give you this information.

God's promises are for everyone. Perhaps you are someone who has lost her way due to being overwhelmed with life, a woman who has been hurt and lost all hope, someone who used to be very close to God at one time but has put Him on the backburner, or just maybe you grew up knowing who God was, but you never developed a close relationship with Him. Maybe you are here and have always been close to God. Perhaps you are like so many of us that have made mistakes that we have allowed to define us, distracting us from our walk with God. No matter your background, I know you are here for a reason, and I know God is ready to meet you right where you're at. He's ready to take you by the hand and show you who you are and what it means to belong to Him.

Whatever caused you to pick up this book, I am so thankful you are here. My prayer is that God speaks to you as you're reading, and that you learn whatever it is that He needs you to learn to step boldly into *all* that Jesus died to give you.

THE BIRTH OF THE COVENANT WOMAN

I had been asking God for direction on my purpose in life. I knew I was hindering Him with my lack of faith because I struggled believing I was good enough for Him to use. This was the result of a relationship I was in that had been causing me to see myself as not good enough. On the days leading up to this particular day, I had been spending time with God, but I was not as obedient to Him as I should have been. I was allowing my personal struggles to steal my focus from God. I was also allowing it to chip away at my self-worth and my joy. My mindset was not in the best place.

Leading up to this, I had been tying my identity to the emotions my relationship was instilling in me instead of my relationship with God. Life was hectic, and when I was spending time with God I was doing all of the talking but never listening for His guidance. The relationship I was in left me feeling like I wasn't enough for the only man I had ever loved. Although he is a wonderful man, and I knew he loved me, we were in different places. His actions didn't always align with my idea of what I believed love should look like.

On that fateful Tuesday, I was seeking God's guidance immensely on whether to stay in the relationship with the love of my life or tell him goodbye. I so desperately wanted to see myself the way God sees me, but my relationship was clouding that view. I knew that He had big plans for me, but I also knew until I started seeing myself differently, I would always hold myself back from where God wanted to take me. It was a woefully confusing time because I know who God says I am, and I could see her deep down inside of me. But I didn't know how to be her when I felt like I wasn't good enough for the man I had been planning my future with.

I told God I needed to hear from Him. With my Bible laid out in front of me, praise music coming through my portable speaker, kneeling on my hands and knees on my hardwood living room floor sobbing, I cried out to God asking Him to change my relationship with this man or change my heart towards him. Face on the floor in the fetal position, tears pouring down my cheeks, I couldn't think of anything else to say so I just waited for Him to speak to my heart. Minutes later my phone rang, and I normally wouldn't have answered given the vulnerable state that I was in, but I felt God nudging me to do so. "Shay?" I heard my mom say. As if she was asking if I was okay. She said, "God wanted me to tell you something. She proceeded, "Remember who you are. Not just the reflection in the mirror but the girl inside of you who lives deep down. The woman you were before life interfered. You are not meant to walk around with your head down feeling not good enough," she said. She continued, "As long as you keep seeing yourself as a burden in any way, you will never be able to use your gifts to fulfill your purpose."

My mom had no idea about the difficult time I was going through. I hadn't mentioned a word about it to her. As hard of a day as it was, her words changed something in me, and I will never forget them. Thank God for my mom's obedience that day. Her words lifted so much weight off my shoulders that afternoon, and I was reminded how faithful God is when we cry out to Him.

God then told me to end the relationship. He had told me before to end the relationship, but this time, I listened. I ended the relationship, only to pick it right back up within a matter of days. I wasn't obedient to what God told me to do. I continued tying my identity to this man instead of who God says I am. I caused myself a lot of heartache and confusion for months and months that God tried to shield me from. I am the perfect example that just because God has a plan for us does not mean we have to follow it. He made each of us with our own will. We can choose to follow Him even when it's difficult, or we can choose the misery of the consequences that will inevitably come from being disobedient. These are not consequences from God because He shows us the path to take if we listen for His guidance. These consequences are from our own choices. The decisions are ultimately left up to us, but He *always* has our best interest at heart.

It took me a *long* time to do what God told me to do, and it was one of the hardest things I've ever done, but I finally did it. Finally, I was no longer waffling back and forth, and God was able to work. He worked on my heart in a different way because I was finally being completely obedient to Him and no longer putting anyone above

Him. I was now giving Him first place in my life. As a result, I grew stronger in my relationship with God than ever before, and He has been showing me who I truly am in Him ever since. He reminded me that He is my source for ALL things including joy, peace, and self-worth. God guided me to pray specific prayers over my future. As I was making God the number one priority in my life, I learned how to listen for His guidance instead of just talking to Him. He's been revealing His plans for my life ever since.

God wants us to choose Him wholeheartedly above everyone and everything. When we are in a confusing or toxic situation, it can cause us to look to other things or people as our source of guidance, limiting what He can do for us. God should be our source for all things. There are times He needs to remove us from an environment so that we will stop getting in His way of what He wants to do. This removal could be for a season or it could be forever but rest assured obedience to God and His direction is key to seeing things happen. We must give God the space in our hearts if we want to see Him move in big ways.

Do you want to know something I love about God? He will always meet you where you are, and He is always patient and gentle! He knows your heart and recognizes your progress. You don't have to be perfect for God to work through you and answer your prayers, but you must have a relationship with Him. If you notice you are not progressing in certain areas of your life, ask yourself if you are being obedient to God's word and listening for His guidance, and then doing what He says to do. If you are not doing your part, then you are most certainly hindering

Him from doing His part. Through the struggle of knowing what to do but not doing it, God never left my side. There were specific areas He was unable to work in my life due to my lack of faith in myself and what He could do in me. This was a direct result of my disobed-ience in not ending the relationship that caused me to see myself as unworthy to be used by God.

Looking back, He told me several times what to do, but I flat out rebelled by not doing it. Although it prolonged His plans for me, He didn't let my foolishness change His plans or purpose for my life. He began giving me insight on this book, letting me know that this Is one of His plans for me as part of the greater purpose He designed me for, but I couldn't complete it without complete obedience to Him. I had started it but never felt it was complete or very impactful until I surrendered everything to Him. That's when He gave me a whole new insight and direction for this prayer guide. I now know this story of obedience was something He wanted you to read, and I believe He will use it to impact your life.

All areas of life are intertwined. I was seeking guidance on my purpose, and God needed me to step out of a relationship to answer that prayer. God wants you to be completely fulfilled in all areas of your life. If you're asking for something in one area, don't be surprised if He works on you in other areas simultaneously. As He was preparing my heart to create The Covenant Woman for you, the first thing He told me to share with you is this...

"You all have crowns because you were all born into

royalty. But, oftentimes you allow the guilt of your bad choices, or the opinions of others hinder you from seeing it. If you don't make mindset changes and start walking uprightly, you will never grab a hold of the royalty you were born into, but it is here waiting for you." These words struck something in me because I could relate to them so deeply. I'm willing to bet that most of us have each allowed a bad choice or actions from another to hinder the way we see ourselves and our future.

I allowed the struggles I was going through to hinder me from moving forward with this book for a while, but God continued to be patient with me. I would often think to myself, "Surely, I cannot help other women when I am struggling with something so big myself."

Here is what I have learned: It is through our biggest struggles that we get to experience the greatest victories. It is what we learn through the most difficult times that allows us to help others. And it's through our toughest surrenders that He works the biggest miracles in our lives.

God didn't put a calling on me to write this book because of what I can do. He called me to write this book because of what He can do through it. He needed it done so that it can serve you, and He chose me to do it. And guess what, because of the in-depth time I have spent with Him getting His direction for this book, I have grown stronger in my faith and my relationship with Him.

God likes to take our weaknesses and use them for His glory. Remember, this when you feel a tugging at your heart to do something that you don't feel qualified to do. If we were qualified to do all that we do, then *we* would get the glory from others. When God puts something on our heart, it's so that He can have the glory for it bringing others closer to Him. When we are unqualified in the world's view, it proves that we cannot do it on our own. You see, this is how God gets the glory and impacts more lives!

Throughout the creation of this book, God has stretched my belief in His purpose for my life and has shown me how silly self-doubt is when it is truly Him working through me. He will do that for you too. He will stretch you, grow you, and bring things to pass that can only be explained with one word—"God".

God wants you to have a deeper understanding of who you are because of who He is. He wants you to know that your past and other people's actions towards you do not determine your future. If you are obedient to His guidance, you will see your prayers answered and your life fulfilled.

He can use *all* things from your past to bring good into your life (Romans 8:28). He used the struggles I brought on myself to teach you and me the importance of obedience. Lift your head, my Friend. You are a daughter of the one true living King, and no matter what you've done, His plans have not changed for your life (Jeremiah 29:11). It's time to pick up your crown and go get what Jesus said belongs to you!

WHAT IS GOD'S COVENANT?

What do you think of when you think of the word covenant? Often, we think of it as stipulations on what we are not allowed to do. For example, if you live in a housing addition, you may have a covenant that does not allow you to put up a fence or have a pet without getting it approved first. When we think of covenants, we often think of restrictions. But here is some good news! God's covenant is *not* restrictive. The covenant that I'm talking about in this book is the blood-covenant each of us have with God as a born-again believer in Jesus Christ. Anything God has promised in His word is His covenant with you. After we accept Jesus, do we need to know our rights? *Yes*! Do we need to make our requests known to Him? Yes! Do we need to be obedient to His word and act in faith? Absolutely! Do we have to be perfect and never make mistakes? Absolutely not!

Our covenant with God is made up of promises He cannot, and will not, ever break. You're probably familiar with John 3:16 which shares one of God's promises, "For God so loved the world that He gave his only begotten Son, that whosoever believeth in him should not perish but have everlasting life." This is a promise to you that God will never break. God's promises to us are love based. He loves you so much that He wants you to spend life eternally with Him! Let that sink in. That is *love*.

Every covenant promise that God makes to you stems from love.

The covenant God made with us in the New Testament does not replace the old covenant; it enhances it, giving us a new birth in Jesus. It causes us to be righteous or in right standing with God by simply asking for forgiveness when we sin. Paul reassures us in Galatians 3:14 when he writes, "That the blessing of Abraham might come on the Gentiles through Jesus Christ; that we might receive the promise of the Spirit through faith." Unlike the old covenant, the new covenant allows us to simply ask God for forgiveness of sins rather than making a blood sacrifice because Jesus was the blood sacrifice. This covenant is a wiping away of our sins by the blood of Jesus, giving us a new life in Him.

Jesus took on physical and spiritual death (*apart from God*) for us when He died on the cross. All we have to do is believe in Him, to accept Him as our Lord and Savior, and have a relationship with God. After doing so we can go to Him anytime we are in need (Hebrews 4:16).

The moment we accepted Jesus as our Lord and Savior, we entered a blood-covenant with God as Jesus' blood was shed on our behalf. Because we are children of God, we are joint heirs with Jesus, giving us specific rights (Romans 8:17). To receive these rights, all you have to do is choose to live by His covenant promises, which means you have to trust what He says is the truth rather than what the world says is the truth. If you truly trust Him, you will be obedient to His word. This is where the Holy Spirit comes in. He is the spirit of truth and will guide you to all truth (John 16:14). He is your comforter, counselor, helper, intercessor, and guide (John 14:16).

Most people do not know what their covenant rights are, therefore, they don't know what is available to them as believers in Jesus. If you do not know what is available to you, you will not be able to receive it. Think of it like this, a friend of yours has made your favorite dessert. She is the most talented baker you know, and this dessert is the one you'll break any diet for and exercise twice as hard for. It's the desert you will always choose above all other deserts. I don't know about you, but I am picturing the biggest piece of chocolate cake with a mound of melted icing on top. This desert is ready for you to come eat, but you don't know it's available to you. It's yours and ready for you to enjoy but you don't know it even exists. You *cannot* enjoy something you don't know exists, right? This means you miss out on what was yours!

The first step is to know what your covenant rights are. Your rights are everything God has promised you. From forgiveness of sin, and divine health, to a prosperous life in all areas. You can find all your rights in the Bible, which was inspired by the living word of God. He breathed the words into the authors. Every word He Himself says is a promise. In the Bible you will find a promise for every need and desire you will ever have. Whatever you are wanting or need, go find the scripture in the Bible that caters to that request. For example, if you are in need of a job read Philippians 4:19 which says, "But my God shall supply all your need according to his riches in glory by Christ Jesus."

Once you find scripture(s) that provide answers to your request, you must believe in your covenant rights. It's very beneficial to write the scriptures down that cater to your needs and desires when making your requests known to God. Every time you put your eyes on it, it will serve as a reminder of God's promise to you. The more you read these scriptures, the more your faith builds, and as a result, you will see more blessings come to pass in your life.

It's your responsibility to not let anything get in your way of receiving by faith what has been promised to you—not the negative opinions of others, not your contradictory words, or even a frustrating situation. You also have the responsibility to be obedient to what He puts in your heart and what His word says. Lastly, praise God that what you've asked for is coming to pass. You do this by faith. Faith is believing even when you can't see it with your natural eyes because you know God doesn't lie.

Taking a hold of your covenant promises requires you do so by faith (as we move though this book we will talk about how to use and grow your faith). Let me give you an example, in my early twenties back in the beginning of 2012, I had just graduated from college mid-year with a degree in education. My financial aid had run out and being the middle of the year, it wasn't easy to find a teaching job. I didn't have a clue how I was going to pay my bills that month. I went straight to God. I remember saying, "I don't know how you're going to do this, but I trust in you and your promise. I reminded Him that He promised to "supply all my needs" (Philippians 4:19). Within a couple of days, I was offered work that had nothing to do with my teaching degree. The job paid me $2,000 which was above what I needed, and it only took a couple of days to complete the job.

You see, this is why we should never focus solely on what we can do, and we mustn't ever put limits on God. If I were to focus on what only I could do, I would have possibly cleaned a couple of houses and made less than $100 or tutored a couple of students and made even less than that. I didn't limit God by asking Him to bless me in a specific way, I just had faith that He would meet my needs, and He did. I didn't go to others with doubt saying things like, "I just don't know how I'm going to pay my bills this month." That would have been contradictory to having faith, therefore, God wouldn't have been able to bless me in the way He wanted because He is moved by our faith. If you are suffering from constant headaches, not having enough money to pay bills each month, or in a relationship where there is constant confusion, you are missing out on what belongs to you.

God's covenant with you is about you prospering in all areas of your life including healing, finances, relationships, and all other areas. There are no limits to God's covenant with you. Now is the time to examine your life. If you are not prospering in a specific area, it's time to change that.

Section 1
Your Rights

WHAT DOES IT MEAN TO BE A COVENANT WOMAN?

Being a Covenant Woman means you accepted Jesus as your Lord and Savior, therefore you entered into a covenant with God. It is important that you understand how powerful this covenant is. The blood of God was shed on your behalf by way of the crucifixion of Jesus... *The holy blood of God!* The Bible states, if you are a child of God, then you are also a "joint heir" with Jesus (Romans 8:17). Being in a blood-covenant with God means everything you have belongs to God, and everything He has belongs to you! How amazing is that? You have access to *everything* your Father has!

The Bible tells us that one of our covenant rights is forgiveness of sins (Ephesians 1:7). As a child of God, you also have the right to prosper in all areas of your life because you live under The Blessing and not the curse. When Jesus died taking our place on the cross, He set us free from the curse of sin, sickness, lack, and spiritual death. When you accepted Jesus as your Lord and Savior, you gained the right to receive the Blessing given to Abraham by God (Galatians 3:14). The Blessing entitles you to abundance, overflow, and God's favor in every area of your life (Deuteronomy 28:1-14). Not only will God supply all your needs, but He will also fulfill your heart's desires. If you are living in lack and bondage in any area of your life, get ready for your life to change! You are a Covenant Woman, and you were born into royalty!

GODHEAD ROLES

As a believer in Jesus, always remember you have access to all that God has to offer, including God the Father, God the Son, and God the Holy Spirit. After making Jesus Lord of your life, not only can you now receive the blessings of God, but you also have access to The Holy Spirit.

The Holy Spirit is a gift many Christians miss out on because they think of God as being far away, but The Holy Spirit dwells inside of you. All you need to do is invite Him to live in your heart, just like you invited Jesus (Luke 11:13). John 14:26 says, "But the Helper, the Holy Spirit, whom the Father will send in My name, He will teach you all things, and bring to your remembrance all things that I said to you." (NKJV) 1 John 5:7 explains, "For there are three that bear record in heaven, the Father, the Word, and the Holy Ghost; and these three are one" (Jesus being the word). God is your source, creator, the one who gives life, your Father. Jesus is your covenant brother, your joint heir, your savior, He is God in man-form. The Holy Spirit, also referred to as the Holy Ghost, is your comforter, your guide, your helper, and the spirit of God living inside of you.

WHAT DO YOU NEED AND WANT?

- God has given us over 7,000 promises in the form of scripture to get ALL prayers answered. Do you need healing? Isaiah 53:5 says, "But he *was* wounded for our transgressions, he *was* bruised for our iniquities: the chastisement of our peace *was* upon him; and with his stripes we are healed."

- Do you need a financial breakthrough? Look at what Philippians 4:19 says, "But my God shall supply all your needs according to his riches in glory by Christ Jesus."

- Do you want to see a miracle come to pass in your marriage? Remember nothing is too big for God. The word of God tells us to trust in the Lord wholeheartedly no matter what (Proverbs 3:5-6). We are to seek His will and direction.

- Do you need to see God move in your child's life? Don't forget that your children are His before they are yours. "'For I know the plans I have for you,' says the LORD. 'They are plans for good and not for disaster, to give you a future and a hope'" (Jeremiah 29:11, NLT).

- Do you need guidance on your calling? Ephesians 3:20 tells us, "Now all glory to God, who is able, through his mighty power at work within us, to accomplish infinitely more than we might ask or think." (NLT)

- Are you trying to figure out what the next step is to take in your business? Stop trying to figure it out on your own. Matthew 6:33 says, "But seek first the kingdom of God and his righteousness, and all these things shall be added to you." (NKJV) It's not your job to figure it out; It's your job to have faith and be obedient to His word.

If you believe in God's word, it's time to stop wondering if you can have your wants and needs met! You serve the creator of the universe, the God who spoke the world into existence. He put each star in the sky and all the oceans in place, and you're walking around full of worry that He may not be able get you the lunch money you need for your kids this week. How silly does this sound? It's time to put an end to these worries in your life. You deserve to have better thoughts than those, and God has already promised you abundance! You must combat those negative thoughts with God's word.

In 2016, I needed direction from God to make the right decision on whether to resign my career as a teacher. A business opportunity had come into my life months before and I had been working on the side. I was loving it but also feeling overwhelmed with the added work.

I had thought about resigning but wanted to make sure I was being guided by The Holy Spirit and not just my own feelings. I looked for guidance and found these encouraging words, "The LORD says, 'I will guide you along the best pathway for your life. I will advise you and watch over you'" (Psalm 32:8, NLT). I said, "Holy Spirit, show me what you want me to do, and I'll do it. I know you know what's best for me. Guide my path."

I thanked Him daily for showing me the right path to take, and I didn't let anyone else's opinions determine my decision. As a matter of fact, I only wanted the Father's direction on this decision, so I didn't tell anyone until after I knew in my spirit that I was supposed to resign my teaching career. It had come time to hand in my paperwork to my superintendent letting him know if I would be returning for the next school year. I felt the Holy Spirit guiding me to mark "no" on that paper so that is exactly what I did.

God is your source for everything you need whether it is finances, or direction and wisdom.

You don't receive according to how fast God can work. You receive according to "your faith" (Matthew 9:29). Are you asking for things you don't have the ability to receive? Can you visualize it? Is your faith determined and confident in God and His word? Sometimes you don't receive an answer to a prayer because you are asking for something you do not have faith in.

Make sure what you're asking for is something you have full faith to receive. Expect a miracle. In other words, if you are sick and asking God for healing, what is your focus on? Are you focusing on your sick feelings or God's promise that you're healed? Can you see yourself healed? If you're asking God for your home to be paid in full, are you visualizing it or still full of doubt that it will ever happen saying things like, "We will never be out of debt."? You must be able to see it to receive it. Get your thoughts, words, and actions aligned in what God says belongs to you.

5

REFLECTIONS

Make the decision *now* that you are done settling for less than God's best. Which areas of your life do you need to see changes? Spiritual, physical, emotional, financial, or relational?

_____

_____

_____

_____

_____

_____

_____

_____

_____

Now, use your faith by closing your eyes and visualizing Jesus sitting right in front of you with his hands out asking you to hand Him each one of these cares. Write down how this makes you feel.

_____

_____

_____

_____

_____

_____

_____

_____

When you start to feel anxiety creep up in any of the areas you listed, remember that feeling of Jesus taking it all away, and let it bring you peace because that is exactly what Jesus wants to do for you. Just remember you cannot receive what you do not have faith in.

Section 2
Ask For What You Want

YOUR SITUATION

When trouble comes, generally our first instinct is to become sad or worried. I'm going to tell you something incredibly important. *You* have authority over all situations in your life. Any situation and all feelings can be changed! No matter what you're up against, *your faith* in God's word can change it. Notice I didn't say God's word changes your situation. I didn't say prayer changes your situation. Often people pray without backing it by faith; notice I said *your faith* in God's word changes your situation (Mark 5:34). Find scriptures geared toward your specific situation and meditate on them. Write them down and read them daily. These promises will bring you strength.

Refuse to fear and cast your care upon God. Keep the faith and keep praising Him through it all because your covenant is powerful even when tested by difficult situations. Is all this easier said than done? Absolutely it is! But when you know in whom you believe, you can confidently write down those scriptures that pertain to what you're going through and say them out loud and proud. Your faith is building each time you do this. This is how *you take authority* over your situations and change them. This is also where peace steps in. Letting God's promises be

9

bigger than any situation provides you peace; it allows peace to fill you instead of anxiety and worry. God is a respecter of faith not people. He is a miracle working God, and like the miracles you've read about in the Bible and witnessed through others, He will work miracles in your life too. If you keep God's promises in front of your eyes and ears, when trouble arises His promises will be the first thing you think on.

GOD'S WILL AND GOD'S DIRECTION

God wants us to prosper in every area of our lives, and His will is for us to have a close relationship with Him. The problem is, I often hear people say, "If it is God's will, then _____." I have been guilty of saying that same thing in the past. We have to stop being lazy. We can find out what is and is not God's will by reading the Bible. It's very plain what we are to do and not to do. To find out God's will, read what His word says.

Now, there is a difference in seeking God's will and asking for His direction. Let me show you the difference. "Lord, if it be your will, I ask that you heal me of my underactive thyroid." God's word says, "...by his wounds you have been healed" (1 Peter 2:24, NIV). Now, doesn't that show me what God's will is? It certainly does! God's will is healing for us all. So why would I ask God if it is His will to heal me? He already said it was. Here is another example, "Father, if it be your will, please bless me with the finances to pay off my car." But doesn't Romans 13:8 say, "Owe no man any thing, but to love each other...."

These are God's words that tell us what His will is; He doesn't want us burdened financially.

Let's switch gears to asking for direction. I can look to God's word to find out what His will is, but when I'm in need of direction, I ask the Holy Spirit to guide me. The Holy Spirit is the spirit of God residing in each of us after being invited.

Let's say I have a business opportunity that comes up, and I'm not sure if God wants me to jump into it. I can read Psalm 37:23 in *The New Living Translation* and be reminded that He directs my path, "The LORD directs the steps of the godly. He delights in every detail of their lives." I would take this scripture along with other scriptures geared towards direction and guidance; I would spend time reading these scriptures and asking the Holy Spirit to reveal what I should do. Do you see the difference in God's will and His direction? If I'm praying something I shouldn't be asking for—that's where direction from the Holy Spirit comes in.

The more time you spend getting to know the Father, the more you'll notice when you have been praying for something that is against God's will. You will feel a halt in your spirit. The more time you spend with Him, the more direction He will provide for you. He will change your heart if you make sure it belongs to Him.

YOUR WORDS

The words you say will either bless you or condemn you (Matthew 12:37). When you grasp the importance

11

of your words, you will talk and live in a whole new manner. What do you want to come to pass in your life? Start saying those hopes out loud and *do not* contradict what you believe in no matter what your situation looks like. You have the God of heaven and earth on your side, and with Him "all things are possible" (Matthew 19:26). God simply spoke the world into existence with *His words* by saying, "...Let there be light; and there was light" (Genesis 1:3). Do you see how powerful words are? Don't say things like, "All the women in my family die young so I will probably never see sixty. We never have enough extra money at the end of the month to put any into savings. My kids are always sick". God's word shares with us that your words will either bring life or death to you (Proverbs 18:21). Stop saying things that you don't wish to come to pass.

Speak those things in which you want to see come to pass in your life (Mark 11:23). Instead of talking about your kids being sick, get in agreement with God's word which tells us "...He healed every kind of disease and illness" (Matthew 4:23, NLT). Choose life-giving words in *every* area of your life and do not contradict them with anything negative. You have the ability to have an abundance in all areas of your life. Meditate on these life-giving scriptures. If you do slip up with a contradictory statement, simply say, "God, forgive me for contradicting what I'm standing in faith on. I rebuke what I just said in the name of Jesus, and I have faith that what You said will come to pass."

In the past, I've said things like, "I get strep throat at least 3 times a year." Guess what? I always got strep throat at least three times a year because that's what I was saying. When you say something enough, you will begin to believe it in your heart, and what you believe will come to pass. I stopped saying that terrible statement, and I stopped getting strep throat. Coincidence? I think not. This is the power your words carry in your life.

REFLECTIONS

In section 1, you made a list of areas in your life in which you need change. Now, it's time to distinguish which areas you need to seek God's direction and which areas you need to find scripture that tells His will. Use the lines below to categorize your list.

_____

_____

_____

_____

_____

_____

_____

Have you been contradicting what you want to come to pass in your life with your words? Use this space to write down life giving words in the areas you need to see a change.

_____

_____

_____

_____

_____

_____

_____

Section 3
Expect Your Gifts

GOD WANTS TO BLESS YOU

That's right, God wants to bless you beyond your wildest imagination. As a matter of fact, as a Covenant Woman, He gets great pleasure in blessing you (Psalm 35:27). Asking God for things is not greedy; whether it's peace and forgiveness, healing of a disease, or a new home and debt freedom. God wants to bless you and give you the desires of your heart, but it's up to you to receive those blessings. *Do not* let others or satan talk you out of what God wants to bring forth in your life. Hebrews 4:16 says, "Let us therefore come boldly unto the throne of grace, that we may obtain mercy, and find grace to help in time of need." So, when you ask God for something, be confident in your asking. It is not about convincing God to bless you. It's about believing in His promises and acting on them.

THE BLESSING FORMULA

When you are standing in faith for something, it means that you *choose* to only believe in what you want the desired outcome to be. This is what you think on. You don't allow other people or frustrating situations to change your thoughts, words, or actions towards what you are believing and praying for.

15

Let's say you are believing God will bless you with a new home. You have been looking tirelessly. It feels like you will never find it. But as a Covenant Woman, you know God honors His word to you so you shouldn't be moved by what you see or even how you feel. Standing in faith requires you not give into your feelings. You continue standing firm in your faith, unwavering, because you trust God. So, if another month passes and you haven't found the perfect place yet, you keep believing God. You keep His words coming out of your mouth and you don't contradict your faith with fear and unbelief. The best way to grow your faith is explained in Romans 10:17, "… faith *cometh* by hearing, and hearing by the word of God." Don't let His words depart from your eyes and ears.

Walking in love is one of the most vital parts of getting prayers answered. As you are standing in faith, you will have people test you. They may say hurtful or untruthful things. They may even treat you badly, but you have the responsibility to love them no matter what, and no matter who they are. The moment you step out of walking in love, you limit what God can do because faith works by love and God is moved by your faith.

Faith + Love + Forgiveness = Blessings

Blessings come from standing in faith.

Faith works by love (Galatians 5:6).

Love doesn't work in an unforgiving heart. (This includes any unforgiveness you may be holding onto including yourself.)

Therefore, if you are holding onto unforgiveness, you are hindering your blessings (AKA answered prayers).

Learning how to be a radical forgiver plays a key role in getting prayers answered. Love doesn't work in an unforgiving heart, and faith doesn't work without love. If someone has wronged you, forgive them. It doesn't mean that you must keep allowing them to hurt you, but you need to forgive if you want God's very best for you. If Sally said something bad about your character or called you a name on social media, should you really allow her to keep you from the home you are working so hard to believe for? Of course, there are harder things to forgive than people saying harsh things, but do you understand my point? Don't allow unforgiveness to keep you from what you believe. satan will use the tactic of offense to try to plant unforgiveness in your heart. Don't let him keep you from your blessing. Forgive and keep believing God's word.

YOUR PAST

Can we agree that we have *all* done things we are not proud of? You, me, Karen, and little miss perfect...All of us! And we *all* have secrets we wish were still a secret from people. From time to time, we try to talk ourselves out of the incredible future God has in store for us due to the mistakes and bad choices we have made in the past. This is a ploy from the enemy to try to steal your joy and your exciting future. He may even use others to hold these mistakes over your head and belittle you, causing you to question your self-worth.

It is time to forgive yourself and leave the past where it belongs! Remember no matter how bad you think the mistakes are that you have made, you have never done anything that is unforgivable by God. Let me make this very clear... you are *not* defined by your past, and God is not mad at you for your past. You are defined by what God says about you. Period!

The Bible reminds us that we have been chosen by God (1 Thessalonians 1:4). Do not choose to believe anything other than who God says you are. God has magnificent plans for your life no matter what your past looked like––20 years ago or 20 minutes ago. Read a few stories from the Bible, and you will quickly find that *no one* God used was perfect or had a flawless past other than Jesus. Most of the time, God chose individuals others would have never thought He could use. In times of self-doubt over your past, simply remember who God says you are and what God says you can do. "I can do all things through Christ who strengthens me" Philippians 4:13 NKJV.

Do not allow the weight of your past to hinder the plans you *were carefully designed* for. Instead ask God for forgiveness when you sin and be specific about it. You're not telling Him anything He doesn't already know. After that, He holds no memory of it so neither should you. Do not carry around guilt for it. You have been forgiven! You'll never carry out God's purpose if you allow the enemy to burden you with guilt or keep dragging you back to who you used to be, and I promise you he will try; he will use people and even try to convince you through your thoughts. Know you have power over him and your thoughts! When satan tries to attack you, put him in his place by reminding him Jesus has already beat him, and He gave you authority over him in Luke 10:19 saying, "Behold, I give unto you power to tread on serpents and scorpions, and over all the power of the enemy: and nothing shall by any means hurt you."

FACT VS TRUTH

People confuse the words fact and truth all the time, using them interchangeably when these words have two different meanings. Let me explain. You may be looking at your troubling situation and think, but this is the truth. No friend, that is the fact.

Think back to your fourth-grade school year. I know for some of us, it's been a minute. Do you remember when your teacher taught you the difference between fact and opinion? Remember her saying that a fact is something that can be proven true or false? A man's height is 6 feet tall. That is a fact. We can prove that, right? Well, in a decade from now, this same man has aged, and like most men do, he has shrunk an inch. Now, this same man is 5 feet 11 inches tall. Facts change!

The fact may be your finances are a mess, but your faith in God's word changes facts, Praise God! God's word, the truth, cannot be changed. We are reminded that anxiety and worry were never meant for us to carry. God's word is very clear stating, "Casting all your care upon him; for he careth for you" (1 Peter 5:7). Did you catch the word "all" in that scripture? When the word of God says all, it means all. We know that God wants us to live prosperous lives because His word tells us so (Jeremiah 29:11). To be prosperous in all areas of life, you cannot be holding onto all the cares this world tries to bring on you. How could you possibly prosper emotionally if you are full of care and anxiety? Thank God for taking away those cares!

The fact could be every spring you get a severe case of strep throat, but that's not the truth. The truth is, "For I will restore health unto thee, and I will heal thee of thy wounds, saith the LORD..." (Jeremiah 30:17). The fact may even be that you, or someone you know was diagnosed with stage four breast cancer, but the truth is found in God's written word. God heals all manners of sickness and diseases (Matthew 4:23).

Perhaps you have struggled with what to do about your adult child going down a horribly sinful path. The fact is they are up to no good, and you are in constant fear you will wake up to a phone call at 2 am from an officer giving you horrible news. The truth is Mark 11:24, "Therefore I say unto you, What things soever ye desire, when ye pray, believe that ye receive *them*, and ye shall have *them*." Don't let the fact discourage you. Allow the truth to encourage you by spending time reading God's word about your child. "Your children will come back to you..." (Jeremiah 31:16, NLT)

Maybe you're dealing with the fact that you are drowning in debt. The truth is abundance and prosperity are God's will for your life, so align your words with His and call yourself debt free in the name of Jesus (Deuteronomy 8:18)! In 2014, the fact of my life was that I was a broke, single mom barely scraping by each month, but I knew God's truth. His truth promised me in Proverbs 10:22, "The blessing of the LORD, it maketh rich, and he addeth no sorrow with it." I chose to believe that and just months later, He brought a business into my life that completely changed my life!

He wants us to be rich or prosperous in every area! You see, God's word prevails above *all*!! Your faith, mixed with His word, will move any mountain in your life—spiritual, financial, physical, emotional, etc. *Your faith* activates the promises of the living God! Use your faith in God's words to change the facts in your life!

YOUR THOUGHTS

Your thoughts hold power and bring forth the words that come out of your mouth. Negative thoughts, or thoughts not of God, can hinder your blessings when you choose to believe them. Maybe you aren't thinking negatively, but you are thinking small which can also hinder what God wants to bring to pass in your life. The enemy will use your thoughts to try and instill fear and discourage your faith. Your thoughts will either limit or encourage you. You can choose life-giving thoughts.

When you start to think thoughts that are judgmental, unforgiving, angry, or negative in any way, bring those thoughts into captivity as you are instructed to in the Bible, "casting down arguments and every high thing that exalts itself against the knowledge of God, bringing every thought into captivity to the obedience of Christ" (2

Corinthians 10:5, NKJV). In other words, imagine yourself taking that thought and throwing it into the garbage
where it belongs. After you get a hold of those negative
thoughts, replace them with what God says about you and
your situation.

Understand this sequence... *Thoughts, words, actions.*
Your thoughts become your words, and you act upon
your words. You must get your thoughts under control
and in the right place so that your words will be filled with
positivity because what you say will come to pass. Your
thoughts, words, and actions will be aligned whether it be
positive or negative. You decide your actions starting with
your thoughts. What you fill your eyes and ears with is
what your mind will think on, and what you spend most
of your time thinking on, you become. Make sure your
thoughts are aligned with what you want to see come to
pass in your life.

REFLECTIONS

Refer back to the list of changes you listed in section
1 that you need to see in your life. What facts are you currently experiencing in your life that you need to conquer
with God's truth?

_____

_____

_____

_____

_____

_____

Now, write down God's truth (Scripture) combating these facts.

_____

_____

_____

_____

_____

_____

_____

You are ready for battle. Set aside specific time each day to read God's truth about your circumstances. This will build your faith in the power of God's words. You are superior to all circumstances when you keep your thoughts, words, and actions in alignment with His words.

Section 4
Have Faith

FAITH

What is faith? Hebrews 11:1 explains, "Now faith is the substance of things hoped for, the evidence of things not seen." Perhaps, to better understand faith, you need to know what faith is not. Faith is not anxious, worried, or sad. Those words all describe emotions that come from fear, which is the opposite of faith. Faith is mentioned hundreds of times in God's written word for good reason, and there are countless stories of God himself saying, "Do not fear."

Faith and fear cannot cohabitate in your mind; only one of them will win. The one you feed and focus on is the one that wins every time. In the past, you have all allowed fear to get the best of you but no more. Those were your old ways. You are learning new ways. You are learning how to move mountains with your faith and get prayers answered!

Whether you have faith that good things are going to happen or that bad things are going to happen, you do have faith. Your faith is a spiritual force that will move any mountain in your life because God moves according to your faith. If you ask God for something but don't have faith that He will bring it to pass in your life, you will never see that prayer answered. Faith isn't dictated by your situation because you know God is bigger than any situation! Your faith can change *any* circumstance in your life.

Are you wondering, "How do I develop my faith?" I'm glad you asked! Just like you read in section 3, faith comes by hearing the word of God. You have a responsibility to spend time with God and spend time studying His word. The scripture is very specific in that you must *hear* the word of God. This means you need to listen to others talking about and teaching His word. There is no limit to how strong you can develop your faith, and *you* are in complete control of it. The bigger the faith, the bigger mountains in your life you can move. Mark 11:24 makes it clear that our faith is vital in our prayers being answered, "Therefore I say to you, whatever things you ask when you pray, believe that you receive *them*, and you will have *them*" (NJKV).

It is your responsibility to believe you receive what you're asking God for. It is also your responsibility to stand firm in faith, refusing to contradict your prayers with your words. Be persistent in your faith. Persistent faith is faith that never gives up until what you're asking for has come to pass. Persistent faith produces results and is confident in God's word. Weak faith produces limitations and discouragement. Your faith must be strong because of the distractions that will come your way. To develop strong faith, you must stay in the word and continue seeking God first above all things!

If you are struggling with fear, make this confession: I am not afraid, for I am the daughter of the King of kings. I am obedient to Him, and He fights my battles. He always wins. Because of Him, I am made to sit in heavenly places next to Him, and He has given me power over darkness. No weapon formed against me will prosper. He created me with a sound mind, love in my heart, and perfect love which casts out all fear. (Ephesians 2:6; Luke 10:19; Isaiah 54:17; 1 John 4:18)

EVERYONE MESSES UP/ FIGHT IN PRAYER

As Christians, we are not perfect and never will be. We will slip up. We will make mistakes. *Do not* let your mistakes hinder your blessings by straying you away from your faith walk. When you slip up, run straight back to God, repent for your wrong doings and keep living the faith life. If you contradict what you believe, simply say, "Father, forgive me for saying that. I rebuke that in the name of Jesus." If your slip up is known to others, and you hear things being said such as, "Who does she think she is? I heard about what she did last week". Choose to forgive those for their judgement and remember God is for you, and what He says about you is far more powerful than what others may say.

Don't pay any attention to the judgement. Their judgement is a sin, and they have no room to judge you. Don't seek revenge or say negative things about them in retaliation. That will surely hinder your blessings. You keep walking in love by being quick to forgive others so that your Heavenly Father can continue forgiving and blessing you (Mark 11:25). Think about what a difference this will make in the lives of those around you—your kids, husband, friends. The faith life is the best life!

PATIENCE

Patience is a vital part of the faith process. Most prayers aren't answered overnight. Patience does not surrender to circumstance. Often, believers give up before they see their prayers answered because they are too impatient and decide God is not going to answer their prayers. True patience is willing to stand no matter how long it takes to see your prayer answered. Even when things aren't going the way you think they should, you have the power of patience to hold you up. We are encouraged in James 1:4, "But let patience have *her* perfect work, that ye may be perfect and entire, wanting nothing." Rest assured that God's timing is always perfect, and He always knows what He is doing. God is working everything for your favor so if it takes longer, you can bet there is a good reason for it.

It is your job to stand in faith, walk in love, be obedient, and be patient as God is working things in your favor. Not only should you practice patience in waiting for your prayers to come to pass, but it is also vital that you practice patience as you are dealing with others; patience springs from love, and love is patient. Do not cave when something troubling presents itself because God is still moving. He never stops moving on your behalf. As you're standing in faith, let patience hold you up.

HEARING FROM GOD

A couple of common questions I get asked is how do I hear God and how do I know it's Him and not my own thoughts? As important as all the above sections are, sitting quietly with God is equally as important. You learn to recognize His voice when you spend time with Him. This is when you can hear and feel Him speak to your heart. Your time with God is a two-way conversation so make sure you're allowing God time to speak to you. If you are the only one talking, you won't be able to hear Him.

God speaks to us all differently. Sometimes through an audible voice, other times a gut feeling, through thoughts that enter your mind, dreams and visions, His written word, the Holy Spirit, through other people, and more. As you are developing your relationship with Him, you won't question when you hear from God if it's really Him. You will know in your spirit that it is Him and no one can succeed in convincing you otherwise. You develop your relationship by developing your faith in Him. How do you do that? By spending time with Him and in His word; you will notice He will begin to give you revelations or teach you new things. He will even open your eyes to opportunities pertaining to all areas of your life as you become obedient to developing your relationship with Him.

Sometimes, He will use this time to give you a change of direction after seeking His guidance on a situation because He knows what is best for you. Rest assured if you are focusing on God's word, listening to obedient teachers of the gospel, and spending quiet time with God after praying, you will hear and feel the Holy Spirit working inside of you.

OBEDIENCE

When we are obedient to what the Lord commands of us, we prosper and live a full life (Deuteronomy 5:33). I learned firsthand that being disobedient comes with its own set of consequences. The Father will never instruct you to do anything that is not in your best interest. God's greatest joy is blessing His children. The quicker you obey what the Lord instructs you to do, the quicker your prayers are answered and the more blessed you will be. He does His part, but obedience is your part. He needs your faith and your willingness to be obedient to make those blessings come to pass.

As women we are often looked up to by our children, our family, our coworkers, and our spouses, meaning we set the example for our loved ones. Therefore, it's critically important that we walk in obedience even when it's not easy. The Bible urges us to be obedient by explaining how obedience impacts those around us, "Whoever heeds discipline shows the way to life, but whoever ignores correction leads others astray" (Proverbs 10:17, NIV). Being obedient in a specific area of your life will open blessings in other areas of your life.

WHEN THE ENEMY ATTACKS, TAKE AUTHORITY

We all have an enemy, and his name is satan. His aim is to steal, kill, and destroy. His number one goal is to steal the word of God from you because he knows how powerful you are with it and how helpless you are without it. He will try to distract you by instilling fear, anxiety, or sickness so he can get your mind focused on a situation and away from your faith in God's word. He will also use people, your past, and anything else to cause distraction and chaos.

The Bible tells us how to handle him in James 4:7 which instructs us, "Therefore submit to God. Resist the devil and he will flee from you." (NKJV) You must remember when satan attacks it is because he knows something great is going to happen for you or through you. He wants to put a stop to it—so, count it all joy when satan tries to stir up frustration in your life.

Know that he will try especially hard as you are growing in your faith because he is absolutely terrified at the thought of you carrying out God's plan. He knows you will impact the lives of others which means he will be unsuccessful when trying to bring them down. He will tell you lies. He will try to stir up confusion in your relationships, your job, your faith, anywhere he can squeeze in difficulty. It's up to you to keep him from being successful. Stay focused on the desired outcome by staying close to God.

The more I focus on learning about my purpose in life and going after what God has called me to do, the more I have noticed satan trying to attack me with the opinions of others, mistakes I've made in the past, and even my relationships. He thinks if he can get my attention—manifested through anxiety, he can distract me from my higher purpose.

31

I unknowingly fell for that tactic in the past. After many run-ins with guilt, shame, and confusion that he stirred up, I realized what was going on. I know God has called me to do big things such as creating this prayer guide for you, and I know satan doesn't want me doing it because it will help other women learn what is available to them by mixing their faith with God's word. He knows he doesn't stand a chance against those two forces combined. Below are four steps I take to combat satan and his evil works, and I can tell you from experience they work.

1) **Put him in his place**. Tell him he has *no authority* over your life or the situation and remind him he has already been beaten (Luke 10:19)! You are a Covenant Woman, and you have been given the authority to rebuke satan and his acts. You are superior to any weapon he uses. No matter what evil act you are dealing with, take a hold of it using the name of Jesus.

    As a born-again believer in a blood-backed covenant with the King of kings, you have the authority to use the name of Jesus to command lack, sickness, and all evil to flee (Philippians 2:10). It has no choice but to bow to the *Name above all names*. Be specific! For example, "In the name of Jesus, pain and discomfort, I command you to leave my back now! You have no authority in my body. I am not moved by what I feel. I am moved only by what I believe, and I believe the word of God, and it reassures me that I am healed" (1 Peter 2:24).

If you're experiencing lack in any area whether it be joy, peace, finances, or health, take authority over it by saying, "In the name of Jesus, lack, I rebuke you. I live under the blessing of God almighty, and I am superior to lack. You have zero authority in my life! (Do not contradict these words.)

2) **God gave you a shield of faith so use it**. Ephesians 6:16 commands us to do our part when we are dealing with evil, "Above all, taking the shield of faith, wherewith ye shall be able to quench all the fiery darts of the wicked." Refuse to fear. Meditate on the truth/scriptures that focus on what God has already promised about your situation and spend no time focusing on anything other than what He says.

3) **Stand on Romans 8:28** which tells us, "And we know that all things work together for good to them that love God, to them who are called according to *His* purpose." Thank God that good things are coming out of these trials! satan has no power over you unless you give it to him by believing his lies. When you stand firm in the word of God and combat satan the way the Bible instructs you to, nothing that he comes at you with will prosper (Isaiah 54:17).

4) **Pray in the spirit and sing praises of the Lord** (Psalm 28:7 & Romans 8:26). This will counterattack the fear and make the devil miserable at the

same time. When you praise God, you are walking by faith and giving Him your trust. It infuriates the devil because he knows his tactics won't work on you. Praise is a powerful weapon against the devil and all evil forces. He will eventually leave you alone at least for a season because he doesn't like getting beat!

The devil wants to steal the word of God from you to knock you down. If He can steal the word, he can steal your faith exchanging it with fear. What better way to honor God and show the devil you're not giving into fear than to offer Jesus the sacrifice of praise even when you're dealing with a troubling situation. Your actions say I refuse to give up, I refuse to give in, and your tactics don't scare me.

REFLECTIONS

Spending time with God and having faith in His word strengthens your relationship with Him. To have faith In His words, remember that Romans 10:17 tells us we have to hear the word of God taught. Seek guidance from the Lord on true ministers of the gospel to listen to teachings from. You can also seek guidance from trusted family or friends.

_____
_____
_____
_____
_____
_____
_____

List specific areas you are not experiencing the fullness of God's blessing due to disobedience? Who else in your life could benefit from watching your obedience to God's word and direction?

_____

_____

_____

_____

_____

_____

_____

Referring to the 4 steps in combating satan, write a declaration taking authority over your enemy in a specific area letting him know you are covenant minded and he holds no power over you.

_____

_____

_____

_____

_____

_____

_____

Section 5
Embody God's Will

WALKING IN LOVE NO MATTER WHAT

There's nothing more important than walking in love. From love stems all the good things God promised us. In fact, prayers cannot be answered if we are not walking in love because faith works by love. James 2:26 tells us, "... faith without works is dead..." Faith is the key to answered prayers. *No love=No faith. No faith=No victory.* If we refuse to forgive, then we are not walking in love.

We are commanded to love one another as Jesus loves us (John 13:34). I am often asked, "How do I love even when I don't feel like it?" Love is more than just a feeling or an emotion. Love requires action so say it out loud. Stop wishing bad things to happen to that person. 1 Corinthians 13:4-5 in the *New Living Translation Bible*, tells us exactly what love is. "Love is patient and kind. Love is not jealous or boastful or proud or rude. It does not demand its own way. It is not irritable, and it keeps no record of being wronged." We are made in the image of God who is love. We were created by love, with love, to love. You don't have to feel it to be obedient to what God has told you to do. It takes time before it becomes second nature, but just like anything else, the more you practice something, the better you get at it and the easier it becomes. Love is one of God's commandments to each one of us, and He expects us to *all* walk in love at all times.

JEALOUSY

As women living in the times of social media, jealousy has become something we are increasingly faced with. In the life of filters and only posting Instagram worthy pictures, it can be easy to compare ourselves and our lives to others. It's easy to post the pretty parts of life without anyone knowing about our struggles. I admit I have been a part of this. The ever-increasing comparison game to other women is a tactic straight from satan. He knows if he can get us wishing we looked like Kimberly or made the money Sally makes, we will focus less on God's plan for us.

When we shift our focus to what everyone else has, we limit our vision and our faith of how God is working in us. James 3:16 tells us that jealousy opens the door for evil to come into our lives. Focus on what God is doing in your life. Have faith in His prosperous plans and be happy for others who He is working through. The blessings God has in store for you will never be given to someone else!

OFFENSE

Let's talk about getting offended. This is something I very rarely hear others talk about, but it is critical as you're standing in faith to have your prayers answered because offense can cause unforgiveness if you give in to it. Offense is a tactic from the devil to mess with your loving and forgiving. Remember when we step out of love and have an unforgiving heart, we hinder everything God is working in our favor.

Luke 7:23 in the *New Kings James Version* tells us, "And blessed is *he* who is not offended because of me". When we become offended, what normally happens? We get angry. We are not at peace, and we say nasty things about the person we are offended by. Is this walking in love? No. Offense will bring bitterness and unforgiveness into your life.

Not being offended doesn't mean not standing up for yourself. But it does mean *choosing* to walk in love and forgiveness no matter what. Remember where offense actually comes from—straight from the enemy himself. Although someone's words or actions against you may be what causes that initial feeling of offense, Ephesians 6:12 remind us, "For we wrestle not against flesh and blood, but against principalities, against powers, against the rulers of the darkness of this world, against spiritual wickedness in high places." Don't allow your real enemy to get you all riled up and keep you from your blessings. Put the blame where it should go and take authority of the situation by putting the devil in his place and continue doing your fighting in prayer.

JUDGEMENT

We have all judged others at one time or another. Here's the thing... It doesn't matter in what way another has wronged you. Repeat after me: *Judgement is not my job... ever!* God didn't want you to have that job or He would have been clear about it in the scripture. Instead we are told "Do not judge, or you too will be judged" (Matthew 7:1, NIV). Verse 5 goes on to tell us that it is hypocritical.

Why is it hypocritical to judge others? Because no one is perfect, and we all mess up sometimes. Do not compare sins. Don't say, "Well I just messed up a little bit so my sin isn't that bad, but Sarah, well, I cannot believe what she did." We have all been there. That is a self-righteous attitude. We don't know everything Sarah has been through. We don't know what Sarah's prayer life looks like. We don't know how much shame and regret she may be living with, and the last thing she needs is another person judging her. *It is not your job to judge anyone.*

When you ask God to forgive you for a specific sin and someone you love continues bringing up what God has already forgiven you for, how does that make you feel? Speaking from my own personal experience, it can be heartbreaking. It can feel like no matter what you've done right, the sin outweighs it all, which is completely contradictory to what God's word says. It can wreak havoc on your self-worth and cause you to see yourself the exact opposite of the way God sees you. That is not what God wants.

Judgement from another can hinder a person's faith walk with Jesus. I think none of us want to be judged by God for hindering someone's walk with Him. Do not judge others and don't allow the weight of someone's judgment to affect you. When you repent of your sins, God forgives you and He holds no memory of the sin (Isaiah 43:25). This is a perfect example of how we should live.

THE POWER OF FORGIVENESS

One of the keys to having your prayers answered is walking in forgiveness. A few years ago, I had a huge breakthrough with forgiveness. I had been holding on to unforgiveness for a very long time against someone who had hurt one of my closest family members. I was so angry and wanted terrible things to happen to the person who hurt her. I wished the most awful things against this person, and for the very first time in my life, I said the words "I hate" to describe my feelings towards another person. I had made it okay in my mind. I took on the mindset that God probably couldn't stand them either. I cringe telling you this because I now know how incredibly foolish, wrong, and unbiblical I was.

In the years (yes, years) following my unforgiveness I started noticing that my life was at a standstill. I wasn't seeing God move in certain areas of my life. I asked God why, and He showed me that I wasn't walking in love because I had an unforgiving heart towards this person, and as a result the unforgiveness was hindering my blessings. Soon after, I was listening to a message from a preacher, who was teaching on forgiveness. "And whenever you stand praying, if you have anything against anyone, forgive him, that your Father in heaven may also forgive you your

41

trespasses" (Mark 11:25 NKJV). It was like a punch right to my gut. It was then I realized that even though God could hear my prayers, there was nothing He could do to answer them because I was choosing to be in disobedience with what His word says.

You've already read, blessings come from standing in faith, faith works by love, and love doesn't work in an unforgiving heart. If you haven't taken time to put this in your notes, I encourage you to do so because it is a sure way to hinder the great things God wants to do in your life. When I grasped ahold of that truth, I was able to see God work in areas of my life that I had hindered Him from working in for all those years that I carried around the unforgiveness. Within weeks my life got so much better! I've experienced the power of forgiveness and the consequences of not being forgiving. I have learned that it is not necessarily about feeling it, but a mindset to forgive regardless of feelings. We hinder God from working and even forgiving us, in other words self-sabotage, when we don't choose to walk in forgiveness ourselves. What we want out of life can't come to pass if we don't first forgive.

No one has ever done anything so wrong to you that you should allow it to cost you your blessings. Am I right? Do you put yourself above God? No, of course you don't. Remember, God has forgiven you of everything you have ever asked forgiveness for, and He doesn't hold any memory of it. In other words, He wipes your slate completely clean!

God's word is very clear when it comes to forgiving others. You do it. End of story. Sister, your feelings will lie to you, but God's word never lies. How do you forgive someone who has done you wrong? You say it with your mouth. Say these words, "I am not moved by what I feel or see. I am moved only by what I believe, and I believe the word of God. The word of God says to forgive so I forgive _____. I no longer hold on to anger towards _____. I have great peace knowing I am living by faith, walking in love, and doing as God has instructed me to do." Say this day after day until you get it into your spirit and have faith in it. After all, what you say comes to pass so keep saying it and eventually you will feel it… I promise!

BEING AN EXAMPLE FOR LOVED ONES

We women tend to want to point out everything that needs to be fixed in other people. For most of us, it has become second nature. Guess what? *It is not our job to fix other people.* I know that one can sting a little bit, but God doesn't want you to fix your husband, your co-workers, or even your kids. Why? We were all born unique with our own personality traits. God gave each of us those characteristics for a reason, and He doesn't want them prayed out of us. He wants to use them for our good and His glory.

What He does want is for us to be the women He created us to be, not the ones the world has transformed us into. As we grow up, we take on the traits of this world. To get back to who we were originally created to be, we must spend time getting to know Jesus. If you want to help someone close to you grow closer to Jesus, you must set the example. Stop nagging them and start showing them.

A few years ago, I watched a video of Stephen Baldwin sharing His testimony of becoming saved. He and his wife had been married for a decade and neither were believers. Then one day, his wife gave her life to Jesus. Stephen watched her grow strong in her relationship with Jesus by spending time with Him praying and reading her Bible. For nine months, she would kneel on the floor and pray daily. She never pointed a finger and never demanded of him. She just fell in love with Jesus.

Guess what happened? He became inspired by the example she was setting. God used her witness to bring him to salvation. Stephen is an adrenaline junkie; God used those specific traits in him to bring others to Jesus, including many children and adults.

See, our personalities were uniquely designed by God. He doesn't want us to forget about our traits. He wants to show others that you don't have to be perfectly polished to follow Him. If you're loud and boisterous, God wants to use you. If you are awkward or shy, God wants to use you. If you are wild and "crazy", God wants to use you. If you have committed horrible sins (which we all have), God wants to use you!

If God only used perfectly polished Christians, He wouldn't be able to transform many lives. Others wouldn't believe they could have what it takes to follow Jesus. Fall in love with Jesus and let Him work through you to inspire your loved ones to fall in love with Him too. It may take weeks, it may take years, but if you keep letting the Lord guide you, you will witness Jesus changing the hearts of those around you.

REFLECTIONS

Walking in the path of Jesus and carrying out God's will involves following the guidelines in the Bible. In what ways from the above section are you hindering your prayers from being answered? Are you holding on to unforgiveness? Perhaps, are you constantly allowing others to offend you?

_____

_____

_____

_____

_____

_____

_____

Do you have a habit of "trying to fix others"? List their names here. Instead of "trying to fix" them, pray that God will guide them and reveal Himself to them. Each day thank God for working in their life.

_____

_____

_____

_____

_____

_____

_____

Section 6
Praise God

MAKING GOD #1 PRIORITY

Do you want to know the key to life? Read Matthew 6:33, "But seek first the kingdom of God and His righteousness, and all these things shall be added to you" (NKJV). This is a command, and it tells you how to have every desire met. It's so simple. *Seek Him first.* It's so important for your faith walk to make sure you are putting God first in your life. Put Him above your family, your friends, your job, your business, and yourself. Put Him above everything! How do you put Him first? Spend time with Him every single day. Make Him your most important conversation.

As a Covenant Woman, you need to be prepared with the protective armor God has provided for you. Hearing and reading the word of God will strengthen your faith and when uncertain times come your way or trouble arises, you will be prepared. Your first instincts will be to refuse to fear and to go to God and His word instead of going to outside sources. You will remember God's promises and those words are the words you will speak instead of contradictory words to those holy promises. Making God the number one priority in your life above all other things will develop inside of you an unwavering faith which will allow you to do your fighting in prayer and without worry, knowing that God is handling whatever it is you are up against.

IDOLATRY

When you make someone or something an idol, it means you are placing a higher value on them than the value you give God in your life. You will know if you are giving something a greater value than God based on how you spend most of your time and how much weight someone or something carries in your life. We are told to honor God which means to value Him above ALL things and people. When we honor God, He is able to honor us (1 Samuel 2:30). You can allow anything in your life to become an idol—music, television, friends, a significant other, your children, a business, social media, literally anything or anyone. Keep Matthew 6:33 at the forefront of your mind, so that you will always be reminded to keep Him first priority in your life.

In the past, I have made the mistake of making people and things an idol in my life. Just a few years ago, I was spending too much time focused on my business while not giving God anytime in my day. I was living to work and putting God on the backburner of life. I would wake up early to get on the computer and check reports and be on calls all night. My priorities were off. I noticed it started affecting me in a negative way. I had become selfish about my time and only wanted to talk about business. My business goals felt like the most important thing in my life. Even with all the time I was spending building my business, I was not progressing. It felt like I was digressing. Numbers were going down, people were leaving my team, and my goals were getting further away.

It didn't take long for me to realize I was in the wrong. I had an amazing thriving business that God had blessed me with, yet I repaid Him by shutting Him out of my life. Once I realized what I had done, I quickly went to Him and asked Him to forgive me for my foolishness. When I asked for guidance on how to do better, He quickly reminded me of Matthew 6:33.

When we get distracted from God, we limit what He can do in our lives. Our time with God should *always* be the *first priority* in our lives. No one and nothing should ever be given a greater value in our life than God. Because He can't work the way He wants to when we don't give Him first place, we open doors for the enemy to destroy all areas of our lives.

OUTSIDE INFLUENCES

Guard yourself against media and other distractions. If you are allowing negative influences to consume your time, ask God for guidance on how to handle it. For example, not too long ago, I had allowed myself to get caught up in a popular TV drama that I had already binge-watched several times. I was getting so sucked into it that when I would wake up in the morning, my first thoughts were about the show because I fell asleep watching it. It went against several biblical values, and God told me He didn't want me watching it anymore because it was consuming too much time and had become an unhealthy distraction.

If you're unsure of unhealthy distractions in your life, ask God to reveal them to you and guide you to what is spiritually healthy for you. James 1:5-7 in the *New International Version* encourages us to go to God when we need wisdom, "If any of you lacks wisdom, you should ask God, who gives generously to all without finding fault, and it will be given to you."

It's also important to be mindful of other outside influences such as the friends you spend time with. Your friendships can either encourage your relationship with God or discourage it. God's word says, "The righteous choose their friends carefully, but the way of the wicked leads them astray" (Proverbs 12:26, NIV). In other words, if you are constantly surrounded by people who don't give God any place in their lives, you will be influenced or tempted in the wrong way and will be distracted from God.

We tend to take on the patterns of those we spend the most time with, both positive and negative. Choose to spend your time wisely. Ask God for wisdom and listen to Him. Ask God to put people in your life that will influence you in a positive way.

THE SACRIFICE OF PRAISE

There is something so incredibly precious about praising the King of kings. Praising Him for who He is and what He has already brought to pass in your life is important. Laying it all out there and worshiping Him for sending His son to die for you, so that you could live an abundant life, expresses your gratitude for what He has already done for you.

When you ask God for something, don't be repetitive. When you ask, believe in your heart *by faith* that you will receive it. Then, every day, or several times a day, praise Him for bringing forth what you asked Him for, even if you haven't seen the blessing manifested in the natural. Praising Him shows that you are living by faith, knowing what you've asked for has already been given to you.

When your child comes to you and asks for something, and you tell them yes but to be patient, would you want them to come repeatedly to you day after day asking you for the same thing? No, of course not. Jesus has instructed us to believe we've received what we've asked for when we pray (Mark 11:24). If we believe the prayer is answered, then we do not need to continue asking for it ad nauseum. Instead praise Him for answering your prayers and be patient as you wait to see it in the natural. This is one way you exercise your faith in God's promises. You may not see it with your natural eyes yet, but God's timing is *always perfect*.

Are you familiar with the story of King Jehoshaphat defeating his enemies with praise? There was a large army coming against him and his people. One far larger than theirs. He and the people of Judah fell before the Lord asking Him for guidance and to take care of them. Jehoshaphat praised God telling Him how mighty He is and reminded him of His promise to rescue His people.

God responded with reassurance that this was His battle and to not be afraid. God guided Jehoshaphat to appoint those who would praise and sing to the Lord to go out before the army. God used praise to defeat the large army who He caused to turn on each other. The sacrifice of praise along with obedience and trust in God's word, and their refusal to fear was how they won the battle! If you haven't ever read this story, I encourage you to read it in 2 Chronicles 20.

Consider times you've been standing in faith on something specific and trouble arises. This can be very hard, but never cave to discouragement. Keep trusting and praising God. This is the sacrifice of praise. Even when trouble arises, you can stay in alignment with what God's word says. Psalm 121:2 in the *New King James Version* says, "My help *comes* from the LORD, Who made heaven and earth".

REFLECTIONS

Honoring God above all things is key to having the life you want and the one He wants you have. Have you struggled with giving Him the time He deserves? What idols in your life are limiting your relationship with God? Ask God for guidance on all the unhealthy distractions in your life.

_____

_____

_____

_____

_____

_____

_____

Is praise a part of your daily routine? Make a list of blessings you are thankful for and spend time praising Him for those answered prayers.

_____

_____

_____

_____

_____

_____

_____

Section 7
Prayer

THE POWER OF A PRAYER LIST

Prayer lists have been something I have been passionate about since I was a little girl. I learned from watching my mom and Nana. They would write their requests down with scriptures relating to their situations and consistently praise God for answering their prayers even before it had manifested in the natural. I remember watching the hand of God work; they were faithful to Him and God was faithful to them. They would stand in agreement with each other's lists just like Matthew 18:20 guides us to do.

I will never forget the two of them standing in faith waiting for their requests to come to pass. They were miracles, both big and small! There was absolutely no other way to explain it other than God!

Even as a small child, I remember realizing the importance of making my requests known to God, standing in faith in scripture, and praising Him even before I could see with my natural eyes the manifestation of what I was asking for.

As I have gotten older, I can confidently say that when I see miracles happening in my life and my family's lives, it is almost always after I have written down my prayers and matched them up with God's promises in scripture.

This is certainly not the only way to pray, but it is biblical. Habakkuk 2:2 and 1 John 5:14-15, shares the importance of writing down your visions and your right to petition (make a request to an authority).

Making my own prayer lists and keeping them before my eyes has allowed me to see so many things I was believing in come to pass. Just a few examples include:

- I have seen many close family members and friends make Jesus their Lord and Savior.

- I have witnessed loved ones healed.

- I have been able to forgive people which I could have never done without Jesus.

- God provided money that saved me from having utilities cut off and allowed me to continue making car and house payments. Literal miracle money!

- We've had court cases go in our favor.

- I have experienced large amounts of debts paid off.

- I have been given business opportunities that changed the path of my life.

- I have experienced time and time again some of the most gut wrenching circumstances turn into some of the biggest victories of my life.

- I have watched people I love completely turn their lives around.

- I have seen friends delivered from what looked like impossible situations.

- We have had relationships mended in my family.

- It's helped me stay on track in my faith walk which has decreased the temptation to fear or have anxiety when trouble comes.

- God has brought incredible relationships into my life that I needed desperately.

The list goes on and on. God is ALWAYS working for you, and His blessings will chase you down if you will have faith in Him and His promises.

Prayer lists are wonderful for multiple reasons. Writing your prayers down reminds you to focus on praising God for bringing those things in which you ask to pass. As you see your prayers answered, you can highlight them. When you're standing in faith for something big, the highlighted prayers will serve as great reminders of how faithful God is and how no prayer is too big for Him to answer. You'll notice the more you focus on building your faith in God's word, the quicker you start to see other prayers answered.

As I was writing this prayer guide for you, one of my closest family members rededicated his life to Jesus. It was not only on my prayer list but my mom's as well. Thank you, Jesus! This is the result of persistent faith and praise. Seeing God work in this way for this family member has grown my faith even stronger.

Just weeks later, one of the people I love most had a breakthrough in their walk with Jesus which was specifically on my prayer list as well. It's important not to be vague, rather be very specific when you make your requests known to God. Prayer lists are also a great way to get the family involved and teach others how to stretch their faith and stand on God's promises.

Here are some things I want you to know. God will do anything you will believe in Him for, but He can't do anything you won't believe in Him for. If you don't say "God, this is what I want", how do you expect Him to bless you with it?

Your time with God shouldn't be a one-way conversation of you reading a list of everything you want. Your time with God should occur throughout the day. It is a fellowship, a friendship. You and God are a team. Let it be a two-way conversation. The more time you spend with God, the more you will understand who He is and who you are in Him. Continue being obedient to Matthew 6:33 by giving Him first place in your life. When you do so, you are honoring Him. He wants to give you your heart's desires, but you must make sure you are doing your part.

You may be thinking you don't have all day to sit down and converse with God. Friend, when you are talking to God, it doesn't have to be a long sit down. It can be 10 minutes as you're getting ready in the morning. It may be the 15-minute commute between dropping your kids off at school and getting to work. It can be 5 minutes as you are folding a load of laundry. Yes, it is important to have dedicated time to spend with God each day; but no, it doesn't have to be for extended periods.

I love getting up early when everything feels peaceful and calm. This is when I sit down and thank Him according to what I have written on my prayer list and ask for guidance on new things that have come up. I also have the time to read my Bible and write down the things He is putting on my heart. Then throughout the day, I make Him a part of *everything*.

Include Him in your thoughts. This is major in developing your relationship. Prayer is wonderful but spending time throughout the day talking to Him is also how your relationship is strengthened. If you had a friend that constantly asked you for something every day but never took the time to get to know who you are, wouldn't that hurt your feelings? Or if you went to your spouse daily and read off a list of things you want and never gave them anything in return, wouldn't that feel wrong? We are made in God's image so don't you think it hurts His feelings when we only go to Him and ask for stuff?

He wants to know you, and He wants you to know Him. If you don't know Him, how will you hear and feel Him when He tells you something specific? Get to know Him. Thank Him throughout the day. Ask for guidance throughout the day. Tell Him how much you love Him throughout the day. Bring Him along in everything you do. Everyone's prayer/fellowship time with God is different so don't compare your time with God to how someone else spends their time with Him. The more consistent you are at spending time with Him, the greater your desire will be to spend more time with Him.

Because prayer lists have helped my family and I tremendously, I am going to share with you how to use this guide to create your own prayer lists.

1. Go to my website www.thecovenantwoman.org

2. Make sure to grab your copy of The Covenant Woman journal from the website which contains the prayer list prompts.

3. Write down all your needs, wants, and desires. Get in the flow of asking God for His guidance on which other things He wants you to be in prayer for.

4. Find scriptures that pertain to each request. You'll find that some requests will use the same scriptures. If you're not sure how to find the scriptures relating to your requests, you can use good ole Google by typing in keywords. For example, If I was looking for a scripture over healing, I would google "healing scriptures." You can also go to the website listed in step 1 for a categorized list of scriptures to meet needs in all areas of your life.

5. Look for 1, 2, or more scriptures that relate to what you're praying for, and then write them next to your request. God will take care of any situation you are going through.

6. Ask God once. Then, every day thank Him specifically for answering each prayer. Say, "Thank you Father for _____".

Go over all the requests just like this, and it will fill you up with so much gratitude for who He is, what He is doing in your life. This will help you stay obedient to His word and direction by not hindering your prayers. You'll show God you trust that even though you haven't seen the answer to your prayers with your natural eyes, you trust His word that you will.

Get in the habit of offering God praise. Never consider this a burden; it should be your favorite time of the day... *you get to do this*! You get to remind God how He is the biggest, most important part of your life. You get to thank Him for what He has done and what He is doing. You get to show the devil who is boss by refusing to fear. As you see prayers answered, highlight them and let them serve as a reminder of how big your God is.

It can be overwhelming to know where to begin in your faith walk with Jesus. In the Reflections sections, you have written down the areas in which you need to see changes in your life, areas in which you need to seek God's direction and other areas you need to seek His will, the facts you need to see conquered with God's truth; and blessings being hindered with your lack of obedience to God's word. Use each of these to guide you in writing out your prayer lists.

Use this whole book as a prayer guide and refer back to specific sections throughout your week to stay on track with your faith walk and build your confidence with your prayer lists. When you are faced with trials, go back and make sure you are doing your part so that God can do His. Your job is to seek God and trust every promise He has made you. Stand firm in your faith that what He promised will come to pass and be obedient in doing your part. This will change your life.

The more time you spend with God developing your relationship, the greater your desire will be to continue spending more time with Him. Once you get in the habit of spending time with God, you won't be able to imagine your life without that precious time. Your spirit will crave it just like your body craves food when it's hungry. Your spirit hungers for God's word and His presence. He is your creator.

IMPORTANT THINGS TO NOTE

A couple of other things that have certainly helped me in my walk with Jesus is taking my problems to Him before I take them to my mom, my best friend, or anyone else. Doing this allows Him to be my source. I talk it over with Him, and I allow Him to take my anxiety away and fill me with reassurance. Most of the time, I don't ever tell another soul about my problems. Why would I need to? Don't get me wrong… We all need girl talk and to be able to vent from time to time, but if it's a problem that has caused me anxiety, I find that the more I talk to others about it, the more riled up I get, causing me to become offended. Stop looking to others to fill your needs. Let God do that for you. He is your source for ALL things.

With that being said, I feel it is important to note that God wants us to help one another. I do believe it is very important to have women who you can trust to pray with you and for you. Women who will give you Godly advice and not just tell you what you want to hear. Women who can stand in agreement with you. Your prayers are so powerful when you are standing in agreement with others, but make sure the ones standing with you are truly in agreement.

I didn't write a specific section going into detail about what is a sin and what is not; however, knowing God's will from reading the Bible will reveal certain actions and thoughts that are sinful. I didn't write a section dedicated to teaching this topic because we are all on different journeys. The more time we spend with God, the more He works on our hearts and shares with us new concepts and teachings. If you are spending time in God's word and with Him consistently, I promise He will reveal the areas of your life you need to clean up. In other words, He will convict you of your sins. Conviction is a fancy word for God will let you know you are in the wrong by making you aware of it. Don't be nervous about being convicted. There is nothing scary about it. Unlike condemnation, which comes from people, and is pure judgment and ridicule, God uses the Holy Spirit to convict us and to guide us into the correct behavior.

Another topic that I didn't dive into is tithing, a way of honoring God with your finances which according to the Bible belongs to Him (Malachi 3:8). I asked God to lead me completely in writing this book, and He did not lead me into creating a section specifically for tithing. I have asked Him several times just to be sure, and it was not a subject He wanted me to go into detail about. Possibly because tithing could take up the whole book by itself. The Bible talks about sowing and reaping. This is especially true when it comes to tithing. From sowing your seed into good fertile soil to doing it with a merry heart, God does want you to know that tithing will open the door to financial blessings in ways nothing else can. As a tither you even have special rights (Malachi 3:10-11). Tithing shows God that you put your trust in Him and reminds you He is your source.

CONFESSIONS / PRAISES

Because your words hold the power of life and death, it is important that you speak what you want to see come to pass in your life. Confessions of faith are a great practice to add to your daily routine, as they help breathe your promises and gifts into reality. Confessions will set the tone for your whole day. I read them as part of my morning routine. These words become what I fix my mind on and when a negative situation arises, I am already prepared with the truth that God is bigger than any trouble that may come my way, and He has given me authority over all situations. Listed below are some of my favorites. You can also find more on my website.

I AM A DAUGHTER OF THE ONE TRUE LIVING KING.

I AM A JOINT HEIR WITH JESUS WHICH MAKES ME RIGHTEOUS IN HIS EYES.

MY BODY IS A TEMPLE OF THE HOLY SPIRIT, AND I WILL TREAT IT AS SUCH.

I AM CHOSEN AND WAS DESIGNED WITH A PURPOSE.

I AM QUALIFIED TO DO ANYTHING GOD HAS CALLED ME TO DO.

I FIND MY STRENGTH, JOY, AND VALUE IN GOD.

GOD IS MY PROVIDER AND MY SOURCE.

MY FAITH PRODUCES CHANGE, AND I SEE RESULTS COME TO PASS DAILY IN MY LIFE.

IT'S GOD'S WILL FOR ME TO LIVE ABUNDANTLY SPIRITUALLY, PHYSICALLY, MENTALLY, RELATIONALLY, AND FINANCIALLY.

BECAUSE I AM WILLING AND OBEDIENT, GOD IS ABLE TO WORK IN ALL AREAS OF MY LIFE.

GOD'S WORDS ARE HIS PROMISES SO I CAN HAVE ANYTHING HE SAYS I CAN HAVE, BE ANYONE HE HAS CALLED ME TO BE, AND DO ANYTHING HE SAYS I CAN DO.

I FIGHT MY BATTLES IN PRAYER WITH THE WORD OF GOD AS MY WEAPON.

I WALK IN LOVE, FORGIVENESS, AND FAITH EVERYDAY.

I HAVE UNWAVERING FAITH IN GOD'S WORD.

I DO NOT SERVE MY THOUGHTS; MY THOUGHTS SERVE ME BECAUSE I KEEP MY MIND ON THINGS THAT ARE TRUE, NOBLE, JUST, PURE, LOVELY, AND OF GOOD REPORT (PHILIPPIANS 4:8).

I AM SUPERIOR TO MY CIRCUMSTANCES.

I AM MIRACLE AND COVENANT MINDED; I AM NOT WORLDLY MINDED.

SALVATION PRAYER

Accepting Jesus as your Lord means you don't want a life apart from Him but one centered around Him. It means healing and forgiveness belong to you as a child of God. After accepting Jesus as Lord over your life, you can use your faith to receive the Blessing of overflow and abundance as a Covenant Woman. If you've never asked Jesus into your heart, and you're ready to make him Lord over your life, repeat the Salvation Prayer below:

Heavenly Father,

I come to you in the name of Jesus. According to Romans 10:9, if I confess with my mouth that "Jesus is Lord" and believe in my heart that God raised Him from the dead, I will be saved. I believe in my heart and confess with my mouth that Jesus died on the cross taking on my sins so that I could live an eternal life with you. I also believe Jesus was raised from the dead causing me to be righteous through faith in Him. From this day forward I live for you. Jesus, come into my heart and be Lord over my life. Father, forgive my sins and guide each step I take in this new life. From this point forward, I am yours, and I want to live my life for you. Take my life and do something with it.

In Jesus's name I pray,
Amen

DAILY PRAYER

Get in the routine of starting each day with a morning prayer to turn your focus to God. Giving Him your first thoughts are a wonderful way to honor Him and be reminded of His goodness.

Dear Heavenly Father,

I take my seat next to you just as your word says in Ephesians 2:6. Thank you, Father, for the love, wisdom, forgiveness, peace, and protection you so freely give; I ask you to help me to walk in it today and every day. When I am presented with facts, remind me that facts can be changed but that your word is the truth, and the truth cannot be changed. As a Covenant Woman, I take everything Jesus died to give me including healing and debt freedom, and I praise you for it. Thank you that you've given me the desire to make my relationship with you the number one priority in my life and for aligning my will with yours. I take authority over every evil force in the name of Jesus because you gave me the spiritual authority to do so in Luke 10:19. I plead the blood of Jesus over myself, my family, my home, my business, my money, my belongings, and every good work you have called me to do. Show me how to be an example for others today, and shine through me so others come to know you. Guide my steps so that your will be done. Lord, please forgive me for anything I've done wrong, and I forgive if I have any unforgiveness in my heart against anyone.

Thank you, Father, for everything you do for me. Thank you for leading me to strengthen my faith each day in your promises and thank you for the path you've designed for me. I love you with all my heart.

It's in the precious name of Jesus I pray,
Amen.

REVIEW

Now that you've finished The Covenant Woman, I'd love to hear what you thought of it! You can do this by writing an honest review on the Amazon listing to help other readers find the best book for them.

JOURNAL

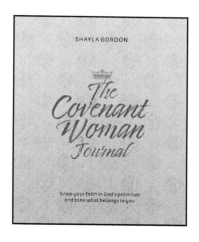

The Covenant Woman Journal is a companion to Shayla Gordon's book, *The Covenant Woman*. This journal provides a space for guided self-reflection as well as tools to measure your spiritual growth. It is designed to help you capture the changes in your mindset as you walk the path towards the life you were meant to live as a daughter of the King. With three months of writing prompts and generous page space for your thoughts, prayers, and scriptures, this journal is the perfect starting place for your spiritual journey to being a *Covenant Woman*.

ABOUT THE AUTHOR

Shayla Gordon is a business owner, mother, and daughter of The King. Through the modeling of her mother, she understood the importance of prayer and having a relationship with Jesus from an early age. After having her daughter at the age of 18, and then divorcing at barely 19, she cleaned houses to put herself through college while leaning on God's wisdom. Shayla earned a bachelor's degree in elementary education, and after teaching for four years, she stepped away from education to follow a business opportunity. This opportunity was an answer to a prayer and has allowed her to lead thousands of women around the world.

Shayla resides in a small town in Oklahoma with her daughter, Kassidy. Being a mother to a teenage daughter and working with women around the world, she has witnessed the power women have when they know who they are and what belongs to them.

Website: http://www.thecovenantwoman.org/

Email: thecovenantwoman@gmail.com

instagram.com/shaydgordon/

facebook.com/shayla.gordon.14/

Tiktok: @shaydgordon

rebel queen

We hope you loved Shay's book as much as we have loved partnering with her in preparing it for you! We are inspired by her experiences and guidance.

With a combined 20+ years in publishing, we know how to help anyone write, launch, and market a book. So if a book is on your bucket list? We're the team to take it from brain dump to best seller.

RebelQueen.co
marti@rebelqueen.co
Facebook and Instagram @rebelqueenbooks